A TALKING POINTS BOOK BY
DR LIZZIE LING
WITH VAUGHAN ROBERTS

ABORTION

Abortion
© Lizzie Ling and Vaughan Roberts, 2020.

Published by:
The Good Book Company

thegoodbook.com | www.thegoodbook.co.uk
thegoodbook.com.au | thegoodbook.co.nz | thegoodbook.co.in

ISBN: 9781784984434 | Printed in Denmark

Design by André Parker

CONTENTS

INTRODUCTION
TALKING POINTS

The world is changing at an astonishing speed.

And not just politics, technology and communication, but our whole culture, morality and attitudes. Christians living in Western culture have enjoyed the benefit of being in a world which largely shared our assumptions about what is fundamentally right and wrong. We can no longer assume that this is the case.

In two short generations we have moved to a widespread adoption of liberal values, many of which are in conflict with the teaching of the Bible. Increasingly, believers are finding themselves to be the misunderstood minority and feeling at odds with where the world seems to be heading.

But let's not be short-sighted: some of this change has been good. Christians have often failed to discern the difference between our own cultural values and those that are demanded by Scripture. We are as prone to bigotry as others. We have much to repent of in our attitudes towards, for example, the freedom and role of women in society, and our lack of compassion and understanding towards those who have wrestled with same-sex attraction, for example.

Sometimes it's easier to protest and rage against the tide of history than to go back to our Bibles and think carefully about what God is saying—holding up society's views, and our own, to the truth-revealing mirror that is God's word.

At our best, we Christians have been in the forefront of social reform. Think of the great nineteenth-century reformers of the slave trade, prisons and poverty: William Wilberforce, Elizabeth Fry and Lord Shaftesbury. But too often, we now find ourselves on the back foot, unable to articulate a clear response to a pressing question of our day. And even when we have understood God's mind on a particular issue, we have struggled to apply it compassionately in our speech and in our relationships. Christians are called to be wise and gentle, even when the temptation is to call out injustices and be rightly angry. The way to approach these issues is to prayerfully and humbly seek to understand our culture and discern the times.

This short series of books is an attempt to help ordinary Christians think constructively about a range of issues—moral, ethical and cultural—that run against the grain for those who name Christ as Lord. We want to stimulate believers to talk with each other as we search the Scriptures together. The aim is to help us think biblically, constructively and compassionately, and not to feel intimidated when we are challenged or questioned, or, perhaps worse, remain silent. This book will lend perspective and offers some biblical guidance on following God and loving people as God loves us.

WHAT THIS BOOK IS NOT...

In such a short book, we can only begin to address the many aspects of what is a complex and controversial issue. Nor have we attempted to present a thorough treatment of all the Bible has to say on this question. But we do aim to give you an accessible introduction to the debate and the many questions that surround abortion. When you have read this short book, our hope is that many of you will be left wanting more. If this is you, we would refer you to the resources section at the end.

But we also want this book to take us all beyond a merely intellectual discussion of the issue to a genuine compassion and love for those who feel compelled to consider abortion or who are struggling with personal problems in its aftermath. We hope this book will be a first step towards understanding the landscape around this issue and an encouragement to know and share the love, hope and freedom we have in Christ.

Tim Thornborough
Series Editor | December 2019

abortion

[a-bor-shun]

noun: **abortion**

1. The deliberate termination of a human pregnancy, most often performed during the first 28 weeks.

synonyms: termination, miscarriage; *rare* feticide
"she had an abortion"

[Source: Google definitions]

"No woman has an abortion for fun."
Elizabeth Joan Smith, Canadian politician

"No woman can call herself free until she can choose consciously whether she will or will not be a mother."
Margaret Sanger, founder of Planned Parenthood

"I've noticed that everyone who is for abortion has already been born."
Ronald Reagan

"Injustice anywhere is a threat to justice everywhere."
Martin Luther King Jr.

"A person is a person no matter how small."
Dr. Seuss, *Horton Hears a Who*

"My frame was not hidden from you when I was made in the secret place, when I was woven together in the depths of the earth. Your eyes saw my unformed body; all the days ordained for me were written in your book before one of them came to be."
Psalm 139 v 15-16

A PERSONAL NOTE TO THE READER

At the outset, we want to acknowledge that you, as the reader, may be approaching this from a variety of very different perspectives.

You may be someone who has a deep concern about abortion as a political and social issue in our society, and is seeking further understanding and clarification of what the Bible teaches and what Christians believe on this subject.

Or maybe your questions are much more personal: you have had an abortion yourself, and there are questions and emotions you are processing, even years later. Perhaps you are considering having an abortion at the moment, and don't know what to do as you listen to powerful and conflicting voices—in your own mind as well as from others. Or maybe you are someone who has been affected by abortion as a partner, a parent, grandparent or a child.

We want you to know that however difficult things are for you now, we believe that God is first and foremost a God of love and compassion. Please forgive any clumsiness on our part in talking about this subject. We certainly don't want to bring you any unnecessary pain. Rather, we long that you will find comfort, healing and hope in the message of the gospel and the fellowship of God's people.

Lizzie Ling and Vaughan Roberts

WHERE ARE WE?

CHAPTER ONE

Worldwide, it is estimated that there are some 40 million induced abortions every year. In the US there are, on average, around 2,400 abortions a day; in the UK, there are around 600.

Then there are consequences. Some experience relatively few, but many acknowledge that they are real and that they can be crippling—for men as well as women.

And then, the bigger questions. *How does God see these things? What does the Bible have to say? Is this how it was meant to be? Is it right?*

We also want to understand our individual responsibility. *How should we support those for whom this is a very personal issue: perhaps those who are considering an abortion or suffering because of one in the past— and can we do it well? And what about campaigning—to raise awareness and prompt legislative change?*

The aim of this short book is to explore some of

these issues as we think practically and biblically about this topic.

Those who are anti-abortion are often accused of adopting their stance unthinkingly as part of a "package deal". Because of their religious beliefs or political affiliations, people may describe themselves as anti-abortion, or *pro-life*, but they don't really know why.

Many readers will be Christian believers. Other readers will not describe themselves as Christians but may be looking to find out why Christians think as they do. We hope this book will enable everyone to feel increasingly confident discussing the issue— whether it's advocating in the public square or simply trying to help friends or family.

WHERE ARE WE?

It is difficult to deny that there is no longer a moral consensus on many of the issues we face today; some would say that we have lost our way. Values that once underpinned daily life are no longer recognised, and we're left unsure as to what is right and wrong—or good and bad.

It's like that with abortion, where there is a wide range of thought and opinion—opinion that is sometimes very strongly held. Debate can be fierce, making it hard to engage with those who hold different views. Often discussion revolves around extreme cases, which, although rare, are desperate and heartbreaking. Emotions run high.

This is the context in which Christians are called to think, speak and act. But it's a hard thing to do and so our default position is often to retreat and keep quiet. Not only do we avoid conversations around this area with family and friends who do not share our faith; we also avoid talking about abortion within our churches. This is largely for two reasons: first, we haven't taken the time to think carefully about the issue and develop firm convictions, and second, we find it difficult to discuss such a sensitive topic and don't know where to start.

The result of this is that we are left vulnerable to going with the flow when this issue affects our lives. When suddenly faced with an unexpected pregnancy, for instance, we are at risk of making choices which we come to regret. In addition, those who are suffering as a result of an abortion are also left without the help and care they need.

As we begin, let's spend some time thinking further about the culture and climate we find ourselves in.

A WORLD THAT DOESN'T MAKE SENSE

The lack of moral consensus which characterises our world today means that as a society we behave in ways which are often contradictory. Much of the time, human behaviour doesn't make sense. This is a natural consequence of rejecting God's moral framework for life—and this means we're now left to our own devices, relying on our own wisdom and making up our own rules. It's because of this that we end up playing what might be called "ethical catch-up".

Consider a doctor who, on the neonatal ward, spends many hours fighting for the life of a child born prematurely. On an adjacent ward, a colleague is terminating the life of a perfectly healthy child *in utero* (in the womb) of the same gestational age. A third doctor, in a clinic at the same hospital, is trying to help an infertile couple who are desperate to have their own baby. Sadly, these scenarios are not unrelated because in attempting to solve our problems, we have just created more.[1]

Contradiction like this is not only reflected in medical practice but in two additional areas—the language we use and the laws we make.

---

1 There is compelling evidence that abortion increases the chance of having a premature baby in a subsequent pregnancy. It may also contribute to future infertility. See page 54.

THE LANGUAGE WE USE

The moment that Meghan Markle, the Duchess of Sussex, announced that she was pregnant, everyone was delighted. It was as if her baby had already been born: the press discussed names and which school he would go to. If something had happened to Archie during her pregnancy, the national and international grief would have been enormous. He was already a child.

In the antenatal clinic the assumption is the same. Parents, absorbed by the ultrasound pictures, marvel at fingers and toes. Is it a boy or is it a girl? What will they be called? What will they do? There's a sense of anticipation and celebration.

This though is not what happens in the abortion clinic. There, too, mothers will have an ultrasound scan. But in this case the screen is often turned away. Without the visual image, it's easier to suppress the truth of what's happening and avoid some of the pain. For similar reasons the child is referred to as a "pregnancy" in conversation, and the act of abortion as "emptying the uterus" or the "termination of pregnancy". The truth of the situation hasn't changed, but the effect of altering the terminology is that the procedure has been sanitised and the child dehumanised—all of which makes it easier to go ahead with an abortion.

Sometimes language is changed out of compassion (even if this is misguided and short-term). Sometimes it is altered manipulatively. Whatever the reason, we must acknowledge that the words we use are very powerful. Subtly, as they are repeated over and over again, they can produce huge changes in how we think. We need to be aware of this and careful about the language we use.

THE LAWS WE MAKE

Contradiction is also apparent in our laws, which have traditionally been based on Judeo-Christian principles. These value life and the protection of the weak. However, legislation has moved away from these principles to accommodate abortion—and in so doing our laws and the thinking that underpins them have become inconsistent.

Historically, the lives of the unborn have been protected by law. In the US today, the Unborn Victims of Violence Act (2004) is a federal law that recognises the unborn child as a legal victim should they be killed or injured during the commission of one of over 60 listed violent crimes. In the UK, there is a statutory offence of "child destruction" for someone who kills an unborn child who would otherwise have been capable of being born alive. The offence carries a potential life sentence—the same as for murder.

However, in the last 50 years in much of the Western world, things have changed dramatically, and unborn children no longer receive the protection they once did. In many countries, under a variety of circumstances, abortion has become legal. And in practice, this often means that abortion is available on demand. In the USA, the case of Roe v. Wade[2] was pivotal in 1973. In the UK, it was the 1967 Abortion Act. Both resulted in dramatic increases in abortion rates.

One of the factors that led to the change was the feminist movement and the desire for gender equality—but distressing stories of dangerous and damaging backstreet abortions were also a powerful influence.[3] Behind it all though, lay an abandonment of the Christian worldview.

In the UK, under the terms of the 1967 Abortion Act, abortion is permitted up to full term if the mother's life is at risk, if she is likely to suffer serious and permanent injury, or if the child is likely to be seriously disabled. It is permitted up to 24 weeks' gestation for much less restrictive reasons meaning that abortion is, in practice, available on demand

---

2 bit.ly/roeversuswade (accessed 11 Dec. 2019).

3 Other influences came from "Malthusians", who wanted to slow population growth, and eugenicists, e.g. Marie Stopes, who sought to use contraception to "breed out" what they saw as undesirable traits.

up until then. Originally in 1967, abortion was permitted up to 28 weeks since, at the time, that was thought to be the "limit of viability"—the age at which, if born alive, the child would have a reasonable chance of survival. This was reduced to 24 weeks in 1990 as a result of the Human Fertilisation and Embryology Act. Today, however, with advances in neonatal care, children are surviving from 22 weeks' gestation and those born at 22-24 weeks are commonplace on neonatal wards, many surviving without complications of prematurity.

In the USA, individual states can place restrictions on the federal law that legalised abortion. Changes to these state laws are often hotly contested, involving lengthy appeals to higher courts.

Internationally, abortion laws vary from country to country, but the general direction has been towards their relaxation and liberalisation. Poland, however, is a notable exception. In 1993, a clause permitting abortion for women in "difficult living circumstances"—which effectively allowed for abortion on demand—was entirely removed from the legislation. In Poland today, access to abortion is much more restricted and is only legal if pregnancy poses a serious threat to the health of the mother, or is the result of a criminal act (such as rape) or if antenatal tests confirm that the foetus is seriously and irreversibly damaged.

TWO POINTS OF VIEW

Generally speaking, opinion about abortion has become polarised into two camps, which can often be heard battling it out in the media and the political arena.

One camp, which describe themselves as *"pro-choice"*, believe that a woman's right to choose overrules any right the child might have to life. The phrase "my body, my choice" describes the *pro-choice* position. It's not difficult to empathise with many aspects of the *pro-choice* position. After all, women carry the burden of pregnancy and childbirth—and often the larger day-to-day responsibility for bringing up a child. Then there are also consequences for the future aspirations of the woman—her hopes and dreams, her career and lifestyle. She might not even have had a choice in getting pregnant.

The other camp is *"pro-life"* and believe that the child's right to life must be protected. Abortion, in their view, involves the taking of human life that in any other circumstance would be called murder. They are not necessarily unsympathetic to the challenges of an unwanted pregnancy and may be active in a variety of ways: in campaigning and advocacy; in counselling (during pregnancy and post-abortion); and in the practical help and education of women, for example.

The *pro-life* and *pro-choice* positions are fiercely held by many—and this drives the frequent and highly contested debates that surround abortion legislation. Those who are *pro-choice* push for legal limits to be extended and are often heard calling for abortion to be made legal right up to full-term so that it will be completely decriminalised. They argue that abortion should be treated like any other medical procedure, choosing to ignore the fact that since it is life-taking rather than life-giving, it is fundamentally different—there is no comparable medical procedure. On the other hand, those who are *pro-life* campaign for legal limits to be reduced and for abortion, except when a mother's life is at risk, to be made illegal at any stage of pregnancy.

The issues surrounding abortion and the inconsistencies raised are important for Christians to think through. *But how big an issue is abortion? Who does it affect?* We will finish this chapter with a brief survey, highlighting why this is such an important topic for Christians to understand and know how to respond to.

ABORTION TODAY

In the UK in 2018, there were over 200,000 abortions carried out[4]—an annual figure which shows no sign of decreasing, despite increased education and the availability of birth control. Further analysis of the figures shows that abortion rates are falling for under-25s, while increasing steadily in the over-30s. It's estimated that one in three women will have had an abortion before they are 45 years old.[5]

In the US, estimates for 2017 are around 862,000, but here numbers continue to fall year on year.[6]

In other parts of the world, however, the statistics surrounding abortion have revealed a different trend. In China and India, where there are cultural reasons for preferring a son rather than a daughter, girls are more likely than boys to be aborted. Conservative estimates suggest that at least 23 million girls are "missing" because of sex-selective abortions in these countries alone.[7] It is anomalous that abortion, so

4   A total of 218,581 abortions were conducted in the UK in 2018, according to Government statistics. en.m.wikipedia.org/wiki/Abortion_in_the_United_Kingdom (accessed 28 Nov. 2019).

5   srh.bmj.com/content/37/4/209.full (accessed 20 Nov. 2019).

6   The Guttmacher Institute estimates that 862,320 abortions took place in the US in 2017. guttmacher.org/fact-sheet/induced-abortion-united-states (accessed 28 Nov. 2019).

7   newscientist.com/article/2199874-sex-selective-abortions-may-have-stopped-the-birth-of-23-million-girls (accessed 20 Nov. 2019).

often promoted as being good for women, is the means by which so many don't exist.

Not only are unborn children discriminated against on the basis of sex but also on the basis of disability. In the UK, part of the reason why abortion is increasing in the over-30s is because women of this age are more likely to have children with abnormalities. So, after antenatal screening (which is not 100% accurate), these children are being aborted. A disturbing fact is that in Iceland, there are now almost no children born with Down syndrome—all those identified antenatally are aborted.[8] Only those who "slip through the net" (i.e. Down syndrome children not identified by screening) get to be born. This should cause us to reflect on what society really thinks about disability.

WITHIN OUR CHURCHES

Since one in four US women and one in three British women will have an abortion at some stage in their life, it would be a mistake for churches to think that this is a problem that doesn't affect them. One American study showed that 13% of those having abortions described themselves as evangelical Christians.[9]

---

8 www.cbsnews.com/news/down-syndrome-iceland/

9 Guttmacher Institute: bit.ly/33QbfAW (accessed 15th Nov. 2019).

The truth is that abortion deeply affects many women in our churches and congregations.

Often, the first reaction to an unwanted pregnancy is not calm and rational thought but panic and a desire to fix the "problem" quickly. Abortion can be a very tempting practical solution, especially in the face of powerful pressures—family size, career, finances, and so on—and the potential for these things to destabilise relationships, marriages and family life.

Although we would hope that other church members would be loving and supportive, many women feel isolated and alone at these moments and find it hard to talk openly. Single women and teenagers are likely to find their situation particularly difficult and feel very ashamed in a church context. And then there are those women who, having had an abortion sometime in the past, continue to live with the consequences. For many, the long-term emotional pain is a reality, and this can be severe.

Developing church cultures where people feel that they can talk about these things without the fear of judgment will go a long way to ensuring that they receive the love and care they need. It will also help to protect the church from the steady drip-drip erosion of the prevailing culture on our thinking and beliefs.

In this chapter, we've tried to give some context to the subject. In the next, we will look at the Bible to give ourselves perspective as we seek a way forward.

WHO ARE WE?

CHAPTER TWO

When thinking about ethical issues, it is important to ask the right questions. Often it comes down to just one or two, such as *Who are we?* and *What are we here for?*—both of which help us think more clearly about abortion. Let's see what Scripture has to say about these fundamental questions.

CREATED BY GOD

The Bible begins with the great affirmation:

> *In the beginning God created the heavens and the earth.*   Genesis 1 v 1

Genesis 1 tells us that God made everything: the stars in the sky, birds in the air, fish in the sea and animals on the land. Christians differ over what scientific processes he may or may not have used, but all agree that God is the great creator of all things—and that includes us human beings too. It follows, therefore, that we should resist every temptation to "play God", as if we are independent, autonomous beings. As creatures made by God, we should recognise his right to call the shots and therefore submit to his authority. That's not only the right way to live but it's the way we flourish: it's always wise to follow the Maker's instructions; he knows best.

UNIQUELY VALUED

At the end of the first chapter of Genesis, it's as if God has a conversation with himself. This is what he says:

> *"Let us make mankind in our image, in our*
> *likeness, so that they may rule over the fish*
> *in the sea and the birds in the sky, over the*
> *livestock and all the wild animals, and over*
> *all the creatures that move along the ground."*
> *So God created mankind in his own image,*
> *in the image of God he created them;*
> *male and female he created them.*
>
> Genesis 1 v 26-27

"The image of God" is a rich phrase which is only used of human beings and speaks of the unique status we have within creation. And do notice that this applies to the whole human race, without exception. History is littered with horrific examples of ways in which some categories of people have been afforded more or less value than others—on the basis of sex, race or class. But the Bible knows of no such distinctions when it comes to human dignity. It is explicitly stated in Genesis 1 v 27 that both male and female are made in God's image, and the same is affirmed elsewhere of every individual.

This is the basis of the Bible's teaching on social justice, and it means that God is concerned for everyone in society, including the most needy and vulnerable. Because God has created every human being in his image, he forbids the oppression of "the foreigner, the fatherless or the widow" or the shedding of "innocent blood" (Jeremiah 7 v 6). The sixth of the Ten Commandments says, "You shall not murder" (Exodus 20 v 13). And when God makes his covenant with Noah, he says:

> *"Whoever sheds human blood,*
> *by humans shall their blood be shed;*
> *for in the image of God*
> *has God made mankind."*   Genesis 9 v 6

The severity of the punishment is because of the dignity and worth of each and every individual.

However, the concept of the "image of God" in Genesis 1 speaks not simply of our dignity as human beings but also of our purpose. Having created human beings in his image, Genesis 1 tells us that God blessed them and said:

"Be fruitful and increase in number; fill the earth and subdue it. Rule over the fish in the sea and the birds in the sky and over every living creature that moves on the ground."

Genesis 1 v 28

We are God's representatives, commanded to govern and care for his creation as we further his purposes for it. How this works out in practice will mean different things for different people (not everyone will have children, for instance), but nevertheless it must surely include procreation—which is why being fruitful and increasing in number is mentioned explicitly. Our bodies, male and female, are perfectly designed for that purpose—to have children.

How does this relate to abortion? Given what's been said in the paragraph above, the act of deliberately removing a growing child from a mother's womb would seem incompatible with being made in the image of God as a woman. We shouldn't therefore be surprised at the pain and suffering abortion causes—it is a profound and significant event.

FLAWED

The first two chapters of Genesis recount God's good creation. All is going well. There's health and harmony. Everything is flourishing. But then comes the account of what Christians call "the fall" in chapter 3, and so much is ruined. Adam and Eve disobey, stepping out on their own and making up their own rules. It's seems extraordinary that they should think they know better—but we all do that.

As a result, Adam and Eve are banished from the garden; they are at odds with each other and with the world around them. Everything is painful and hard—from having and raising children to working the ground and finding food. Corrupted to its core, life is no longer how it was meant to be.

It is the fall that is behind all that's wrong with the world—including abortion and the reasons women might feel the need to have one. If we were not fallen, poverty and oppressive patriarchy wouldn't exist; attitudes to sex, relationships and family life wouldn't leave women unsupported and sometimes abused; and cultural expectations of many kinds wouldn't exert seemingly irresistible pressures.

Not only is the fall behind fractured relationships and unjust cultural practices; it also lies behind how we view ourselves as persons. Western contemporary thought has been heavily influenced by Descartes, the 17th-century French philosopher whose dualistic philosophy dissociated our minds from our bodies. He coined the phrase "I think; therefore I am", although similar ideas can be traced back to the Gnosticism of the first and second centuries, and beyond that to Plato. A more modern catchphrase that channels the same idea is "I am not my body". Both phrases reflect the fact that in our thinking and unconscious assumptions, we separate our "true selves" from our physical bodies. In fact, our bodies are relegated to being an inferior component, which is no longer part of the real "me". Our true identity is, they say, in our minds—or, we might say "in our souls".[10]

This disintegration of our identity (splitting apart our mind, body and soul) has had wide-ranging and damaging consequences. In philosophical thought it is reflected in a view of personhood which has been used to justify abortion and infanticide as well as euthanasia. We'll look at that further in the next chapter. But on a personal level, it means that we tend to think that we have a right to do what we want with our bodies—and that we should be able to do so without consequences. But that's not the case. Many testify to significant mental and emotional trauma after an abortion: one woman described her abortion as having left her feeling "stripped".

The all-pervasive effect of the fall means that, when thinking about abortion, we need to acknowledge that the issue is complex and multifaceted. We will come back to this in chapter 4, but first, we'll look further at the ethics of abortion.

---

10 See Nancy Pearcey, *Love Thy Body* (Baker Books, 2018).

BETH'S STORY

I was 19 when I went to university, and soon after I got there, I met my first boyfriend. I was madly in love and after being with him for six months, I found out I was pregnant. This wasn't something I'd planned, and my reactions swung between "Wow, this is amazing" and "S*@%! Mum is going to go mad".

I really think there would have been a good chance of my keeping the child—an abortion wasn't inevitable. However, I'd never forgotten the way my mum had responded when my older sister, who wasn't married, got pregnant and had her son. She pushed her away; went on and on about how stupid she'd been. My dad too. "Well, that's her life over," he said. "What will so-and-so think? Will we ever live this down?" The shame they felt was palpable, and I was about to add to it. On top of that my father had just retired on the grounds of ill-health, and this was the last thing he needed. And so, I decided to have an abortion.

It was not something I took lightly at the time. I think I knew it was wrong back then. Today, I'm sure I should never have done it, and I wish I hadn't. One way or another the shame of it has hung over my life ever since. I'm now 46. Sometimes, when I see a baby or a small child, I'm reminded of the child I might have had. I wonder what he or she would have been like. I could have been a grandmother by now.

But despite regret and shame, I have hope. When I am reminded of what I have done (and it was, at the end of the day, my decision), I remember that Jesus has died for me. He loves me despite what I have done. I am completely forgiven. And for that I am very, very grateful. One day, I will meet him face to face. I am also filled with hope that I will meet my child because I know that God loved him/her—even though I chose not to.

WHEN ARE WE HUMAN?

CHAPTER THREE

The *Who are we?* question, which we have just considered, is crucial. However, discussion and debate around abortion often focuses on a different question: *When do we become human?* This is an important question because much of the abortion debate hinges on whether the embryo/foetus can be considered to have life and if it does, whether it can be considered a person with rights.

THE SCIENCE OF LIFE

From the perspective of pure science, there is no doubt that a distinct human life begins at conception. When a sperm fertilises an egg, 23 chromosomes from the mother and 23 from the father combine to produce a completely new, genetically unique single cell (zygote). This zygote contains all the genetic information required to produce all the features and functions of a mature human being.[11] It's worth taking a minute to stop and think about how amazing this is. Each zygote is different to any other.

From the time of fertilisation, a new, distinct human being comes into existence, and then over weeks and months and years gradually he or she will develop into a fully grown adult:

- As early as four weeks,[12] the embryonic heart, although not yet fully formed, begins to beat; blood-cell production has already begun; the head can be distinguished from the body and early arms, legs, ears and eyes start to appear.
- At six weeks, hands, feet, fingers and toes are visible on an ultrasound scan. The face is developing with rudimentary sinuses, mouth and nose.
- By eight weeks, the heart is fully formed, milk teeth are present, and the embryo is starting to produce its own hormones. All essential external and internal structures are in place, and in recognition of this, the embryo is now called a foetus.

---

11 And occasionally two—in the case of identical twins.

12 That is, four weeks from fertilisation. This is different to gestational age, which is the traditional method of estimating pregnancy length and is counted from the first day of the last period. To translate the number used here, add two weeks to arrive at the gestational age.

All that's now necessary for a foetus to become a mature human being is a suitable environment, food and time. Birth does nothing to change those needs—only the way in which they're provided.

Alexander Tsiaras is a medical-imaging specialist who has pioneered new ways of visualising babies *in utero*. His TED talk, which includes verifiable video material based on micro-MRI scanning, is well worth watching.[13] It charts the extraordinary development of the structures of the human body from conception to birth. For Tsiaras, the complexities contained within the genetic code as egg and sperm come together, are mind-blowing. Despite his intellect and genius, all he can say is: "It's mystery, it's magic, it's divinity". It is truly amazing.

COMPETING RIGHTS

Both *pro-life* and *pro-choice* lobbies believe that women have rights, but they differ as to whether the child *in utero* also has rights. Some believe we should regard the human embryo/foetus, at least in the earliest stages of its development, as simply being a part of the woman's body and therefore hers to do with as she wishes—and so the issue is focused only on the woman's right to choose. But it is a very different matter if the embryo/foetus is understood

13 TED: bit.ly/2qhJCC5 (accessed 15th November 2019).

to be a distinct human life. Surely then we would need to recognise that it has rights too.

Antonia Senior, a British journalist, admits that having her own baby challenged her strongly held pro-abortion views. She knew that her daughter had been formed at conception and writes:

> *Any other conclusion is a convenient lie that we on the pro-choice side of the debate tell ourselves to make us feel better about the action of taking a life.*

Nevertheless, as she continues her argument, she comes to sinister conclusions as women's rights are played off against the rights of the unborn. "The single biggest factor in women's liberation," she says, "was our newly found ability to impose our will on our biology … The nearly 200,000 aborted babies in the UK each year are the lesser evil, no matter how you define life." She concludes by saying that to defend women's rights, "You must be prepared to kill".[14]

There is a brutal honesty in those words; Senior is honest enough to face up to the scientific evidence. But the shocking reality is that she then allows one group to trump the rights of the other—and it can only do that because it has power which the other does not. The oppressed have become the oppressors.

---

14 *The Times:* bit.ly/32MwbqX (accessed 15th November 2019).

WE ARE KNOWN

> [13]*For you created my inmost being;*
> *you knit me together in my mother's womb.*
> [14]*I praise you because I am fearfully and*
> *wonderfully made;*
> *your works are wonderful,*
> *I know that full well.*
>
> [15]*My frame was not hidden from you*
> *when I was made in the secret place,*
> *when I was woven together in*
> *the depths of the earth.*
> [16]*Your eyes saw my unformed body;*
> *all the days ordained for me were*
> *written in your book*
> *before one of them came to be.*
>
> [17]*How precious to me are your thoughts, God!*
> *How vast is the sum of them!*
> [18]*Were I to count them, they would outnumber*
> *the grains of sand—*
> *when I awake, I am still with you.*
>
> Psalm 139 v 13-18

Psalm 139 is a beautiful psalm and it would be good to have a Bible open at this point as we look not only at the verses above but also at those that go before and come afterwards. Read through the whole psalm now and then follow along, as you read through the next few paragraphs. It will be well worth the effort.

The tone of this poem is one of awe and amazement. David (the songwriter) is overwhelmed by just how deeply and intimately God knows him—so deeply and intimately that it's impossible to fathom (v 6). There is nowhere he can go where God won't hold him fast (v 10). He is safe. He is secure—hemmed in "behind and before" (v 5) by God's knowledge of him and his presence with him.

And what David knows to be true in the present he also knows to be true of the past—because even as an embryo ("unformed body"—v 16), God knew him. He was with him even then—as he knit him together in his mother's womb. And, just as God knows what the adult David is going to say before he says it (v 4), God knew what lay ahead for David even when he was still in the womb (v 16).

In verses 17-18, David is amazed—he can't quite take it all in. But then, having cast his mind back to the very beginning of his life (conception—v 16), he now looks forward to the resurrection (v 18) when he will "awake" from the sleep of death into the fullness of eternal life. In the past, present and future, David knows that God is with him, and that he is intimately known by him. Created by God, David is David—in the womb, out of the womb and even beyond death.

While God knew David before he was born, the

relationship was clearly not reciprocal—an embryo's ability to respond to God's love is severely limited. Rather, we grow in our knowledge and love of God over the course of our lives, having put our faith in Jesus Christ. Only at the resurrection will we know God as he has always known us. In the New Testament, the Apostle Paul says this:

> *For now we see only a reflection as in a mirror; then we shall see face to face. Now I know in part; then I shall know fully, even as I am fully known.*   1 Corinthians 13 v 12

The final six verses of Psalm 139 can come as a bit of a shock but, nevertheless, they make sense in view of what's gone before. With lofty thoughts of God going through his mind, it's as if David is suddenly struck by all that's going on around him. It's not right and he's justly angry at those who rebel against God and do evil—and in the final couple of verses, he turns his thoughts to himself, asking God to help him see his own faults and guide him into eternal life (v 24).

There are other texts that point to our existence as individuals from conception—or even before. In Jeremiah 1 v 5, for example, God says to Jeremiah, "Before I formed you in the womb I knew you" – and in Judges 13 v 5, God says to Samson's mother, "You will become pregnant and have a son whose head is never to be touched by a razor because the boy is to be a Nazirite, dedicated to God from the womb". Verses like these illustrate that a child in the womb not only has "biological life" but also a God-given individual identity from conception.

THE HUMANITY OF JESUS

In the New Testament, the writer of the letter to the Hebrews reminds us that when Jesus left heaven for earth, he was made "fully human in every way". And so, for the purposes of our current discussion, a good question to ask would be "When did Jesus become human?"

Within the church, there has never been any doubt: Jesus was incarnate (that is, he is the eternal God who became a human being) at his conception when, as the Angel Gabriel promised Mary, the Holy Spirit "came over" her and the power of the Most High "overshadowed her". (Luke 1 v 35). Christians would never deny that this, as opposed to his birth, was when Jesus became man.

As if to illustrate this, the Gospel-writer Luke goes on to describe Mary's visit to see her elderly relative Elizabeth. Mary is in the early stages of pregnancy with Jesus: Elizabeth is significantly further on, carrying John the Baptist. Mary and Elizabeth already know that Jesus is the Saviour of the world—but the one who would prepare the way for Jesus, John the Baptist, even *in utero*, seems to sense something of that too. Here is how the event is described in Luke's Gospel:

> *At that time Mary got ready and hurried to a town in the hill country of Judea, where she entered Zechariah's home and greeted Elizabeth. When Elizabeth heard Mary's greeting, the baby leaped in her womb, and Elizabeth was filled with the Holy Spirit. In a loud voice she exclaimed: "Blessed are you among women and blessed is the child you will bear! But why am I so favoured, that the mother of my Lord should come to me? As soon as the sound of your greeting reached my ears, the baby in my womb leaped for joy.*
>
> Luke 1 v 39-44

Commentating on this passage, John Wyatt says:

> *I have sometimes wondered why, out of all the eyewitness accounts of Jesus' life that Luke must have accumulated before he wrote his Gospel, did he choose to record such a commonplace domestic incident. Was it because Luke wanted to emphasise that Jesus' earthly ministry commenced even before birth? At first glance there are only two people in that room in*

Zechariah's home. But Luke implies that there are in fact four. Elizabeth and the unborn John, Mary and the unborn Jesus, And perhaps what captivated Luke was the recognition that John leapt for joy at Jesus' presence, only a few weeks after his conception, in the same way that lepers and paralysed men and blind beggars will leap for joy as Jesus passes by in future.[15]

There is continuity before birth and after birth which the Bible takes for granted—it's just how it is.[16] But this continuity goes further and continues after Jesus' death. Jesus, now resurrected, ascended and seated at the right hand of the Father, is still fully human as he intercedes for us.

In the words of the Apostles Creed:

He [Jesus] was conceived by the Holy Spirit,
born of the Virgin Mary,
suffered under Pontius Pilate,
was crucified, died and was buried .
On the third day he rose again.

The same person from conception to resurrected glory.

---

15 John Wyatt, *Matters of Life and Death* (IVP, 2009) p 162.

16 Consider, for example, the Greek word *Brephos* which is translated as baby or child: It is used in Luke 1 v 41, 44 to describe John the Baptist *in utero*; in Luke 2 v 12, 16 to refer to the new-born Jesus and in Luke 18 v 15 to the little children brought to Jesus.

PERSONHOOD ARGUMENTS

The concept of personhood has deep theological roots which go right back to the very beginnings of the Bible and to the heart of God himself: Father, Son and Holy Spirit—one God in three Persons. And for human beings, made in the image of God, this means that to be human is to have personhood.

However, many in our world see things differently and seek to separate our humanity from our personhood. While accepting that abortion is the taking of a human life, they justify it by arguing that the embryo does not merit the status of a person. Dr Megan Best writes:

> We no longer need to argue in informed circles that human embryos are indeed embryonic humans. The question we now face in public policy is this: at what stage of development does the nascent human life deserve protection ... The proponents of destructive embryo research and abortion usually advocate that protection is only due to human persons, and that personhood is not conferred merely on biological grounds. The modern idea is that the status of "personhood" is not automatically given to any human being, but only to those who can perform certain functions.[17]

17 *Fearfully and Wonderfully Made* (Matthias Media, 2012) p 31-32.

So, the debate is no longer about *when* life begins but whether that life is worthy of protection. In practice, there are a variety of views as to when personhood is achieved and what constitutes relevant functions, abilities or capacities. For some, personhood begins at implantation, when, six days after fertilisation, the embryo becomes attached to the wall of the uterus and is in an environment where maturation will occur. For others, personhood begins at the point of viability when, if born prematurely, the foetus would have a reasonable chance of survival. Yet others say that personhood begins at birth when the baby becomes physically independent from the mother.

Alternatively, some argue that the capacities that confer personhood may be non-physical ones such as the ability to reason and act intentionally, to communicate and relate to others, or to be conscious and self-aware.

You will notice that these ideas of personhood are quite a shift from the perspective we've taken in this book. Instead of our identity and moral status being conferred on us when we were made in the image of God, contemporary arguments require us to have lived long enough or to have met certain criteria in order to have worth.

If, as is proposed, personhood depends on the attainment of certain criteria, we are bound to ask who sets them and on what basis. There are various views. Peter Singer, Professor of Bioethics at Princeton University, has defined a person as "a rational and self-aware being"[18]—one who has preferences and is able to make decisions. On that basis some primates are persons, but some human beings are not, either because they are not fully developed (like a baby in the womb) or because they have impaired capacities (because of congenital conditions, illness or ageing, for example). It is no surprise that Singer supports abortion, euthanasia and, in some conditions, infanticide.

James Watson, one of those credited with discovering the DNA double helix, has argued that because some defects are only discovered after birth, it should be possible to kill babies in their first three days of life. Others have argued for what they call "post-birth abortion" so that killing an infant would be permissible in all the cases where abortion is.[19] Peter Singer has suggested that even a three-year-old is "a grey case".[20]

These examples illustrate the slippery slope of today's personhood arguments. It's no wonder that disability advocates, in particular, are profoundly

---

18 Peter Singer, *Practical Ethics* (CUP, 2011), p 75.

19 jme.bmj.com/content/39/5/261 (accessed 28 Nov. 2019).

20 religion-online.org/article/who-lives-who-dies-the-utility-of-peter-singer (accessed 28 Nov. 2019).

disturbed by such reasoning, the implication being that the lives of those with significant disability have less value, if they are worthy of life at all. But the Bible presents a very different understanding. Our dignity as human beings or human persons is inherent and not earned. All people, without exception, have great value because they have been made in the image of God. And this is not dependent on our age or abilities, but simply on the God who made us, knew us and loved us—even from the moment of our conception.

A COMPLEX ISSUE

CHAPTER FOUR

There have been huge changes in recent decades and abortion is now widely practised. We need to ask *Why has this happened?* and *How has it come about?* Our answers to these questions will help shape our responses to two further questions: *What can we do?* and *How can we help?* These are good questions to ask.

ROOT CAUSES

Abortion is a complex and multifaceted issue and so it's not surprising that there are many underlying factors that have led to the situation we find ourselves in today. Some of these are shown in the diagram on the next page—which is offered as a tool to help us think and discuss. There are undoubtedly other factors not included here, but hopefully these are a good starting point.

POSSIBLE CONSEQUENCES

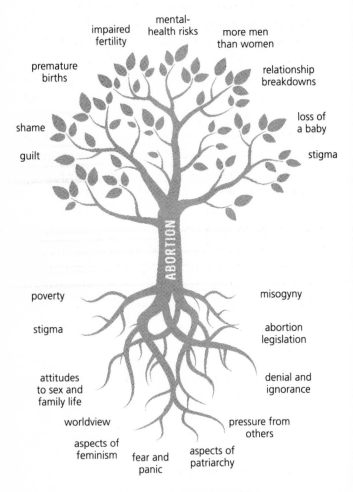

impaired
fertility

mental-
health risks

more men
than women

premature
births

relationship
breakdowns

shame

loss of
a baby

guilt

stigma

ABORTION

poverty

misogyny

stigma

abortion
legislation

attitudes
to sex and
family life

denial and
ignorance

worldview

pressure from
others

aspects of
feminism

fear and
panic

aspects of
patriarchy

POSSIBLE ROOT CAUSES

As we look at the root causes mentioned, it's important to acknowledge that things are not always clear-cut. Consider the influence of the feminist movement, for example. Rightly understood, there has been much that's been good about feminism. It has challenged great injustices in the past and continues to speak out against misogyny and oppressive patriarchy today. But it's not all good: second-wave feminism took a turn in the 1960s in its quest for reproductive freedom. In attempting to liberate women from how they were biologically created, feminism has had profound and detrimental consequences ever since—not only for women but also for the unborn child.

Not only do root causes play out in wider society, but they can be powerfully influential at a personal level too. Consider these comments gleaned from the experience of a variety of women:

> *"I was scared and ashamed. I didn't feel I had any control or choice."*

> *"His dad doesn't want him, and I can't do this all by myself."*

> *"He said he'd beat the baby out of me unless I had an abortion."*

> *"If only we hadn't slept together."*

"I had been brought from India for an arranged marriage. My problems started when I became pregnant and the scan revealed that I was expecting a girl baby."

Just as abortion is a complex societal issue, it is often very difficult and complex at a personal level too. Women who have an abortion often feel they have no choice, even if they don't think it's right.

POSSIBLE CONSEQUENCES

There is much debate between *pro-life* and *pro-choice* groups about the risks and complications of abortion—whether there are any and what they might be. What evidence there is can be biased and difficult to assess, and so is hotly contested. Nevertheless, in some areas it is undeniably compelling.[21] There seems little doubt, for instance, that the practice of abortion is a contributory factor in infertility, recurrent miscarriage and premature birth. Each one of these medical issues has significant consequences of its own—potentially for individuals but certainly for society as a whole. Debate continues around mental-health issues and breast cancer. Few women however, are left completely

---

21 A useful resource on this is *Complications: Abortion's Impact on Women* (deVeber, 2013). See also this briefing paper from the Christian Medical Fellowship bit.ly/2CKIGJb (accessed 15th Nov. 2019).

unscathed by an abortion. Men, too, are not unaffected. Consider these comments:

"I was 16 when I found out my girlfriend was pregnant. She decided it wasn't time and chose an abortion, leaving me heartbroken."

"My wife does not want the baby and wants to focus on her career. I have said I will support her decision, but I would dearly love to keep the child."

"After the abortion we ended up separating. Yet I sensed I was not the same. There was a sense of grief and shame in my life that clung to me even though I tried to shrug it off."

WHAT CAN WE DO?

Thinking about the root causes and possible consequences of abortion can help us see where and how we could get involved. We could, for instance, work to prevent abortion or to mitigate its effects. We could focus on the support and care of women, or advocate for the rights of the unborn.

Given the injustice of abortion, speaking out on the issue is important, but there are various ways of doing this: simply talking to others and making them aware of what's going on; adding our voice to public debate on abortion and other related issues;

or challenging political representatives and taking part in peaceful protests. It can be helpful to sign up for email alerts from advocacy groups so that we can pray into current political (and pastoral) situations.

But campaigning on its own can never be enough. The complexities of the abortion issue demand a breadth of response. Women in difficult situations need help and support—as do families under pressure as they seek to raise children. And when others are suffering as a result of abortion, we need to find a way to love and serve them with sensitivity and compassion.

Our response should also include the adoption and fostering of children whose mothers have carried them to term but who are unable to give them a home. Those who are *pro-choice* often complain that *pro-lifers* are really just "pro-birthers"—so long as the child is born, then that is their job done. The truth is that that can never be a fully Christian position.

Various well-established *pro-life* organisations exist—not just to campaign but also to help and support women and families. They may or may not have a religious foundation. Many are doing excellent work and are involved in a variety of areas: emergency helplines; counselling (pregnancy and post-abortion); safe houses and skills training for vulnerable women; campaigning and advocacy;

awareness-raising and education, as well as research. Often, they welcome and train volunteers.[22]

Whether or not we decide to formally get involved with such agencies, we will all have informal opportunities to speak about abortion and care for those affected. This is the focus of the next two chapters.

JENNY'S STORY

When a woman is facing an unintended pregnancy, it can feel as if her world has been turned upside down, and there often follows a struggle between what her head is telling her and what her heart is saying. Sadly, today more often than not the head wins, and the emotions of the heart must be suppressed to enable the woman to continue with her life. For many, there will come a time when these emotions rise to the surface: post-abortion hurts and struggles are very real.

I have had the privilege of working for many years with those affected by unintended pregnancy and post-abortion concerns—both in the community and in our church families. Those who seek our help can find forgiveness, and healing, and a purpose for their lives by working through a post-abortion recovery programme so that we can move on with hope and

22 Life (www.lifecharity.org.uk) is a good example in the UK.

trust for the future. We give ourselves permission to grieve, like any mother or father grieving the loss of their baby, and consider both extending and receiving forgiveness.

While spending time in a church the US, I visited a lady who, with great courage and many tears, had attended our post-abortion healing group. At the side of the road leading into her town was a huge banner which read, "Abortion stops a beating heart". I asked her how she had felt, with her secret guilt and grief of over 30 years, driving past that banner each day. She replied that she had learned to harden her heart to it as she knew only too well the deep pain of having made that decision which ended her baby's life. She later reflected more on this and said, "Jenny, it is true that abortion stops a beating heart. But here is one step further: who will care for the hearts that remain beating but broken?" This is the message that God calls us to share: Jesus came to heal the broken-hearted.

ENGAGING PRACTICALLY: GUIDING PRINCIPLES

CHAPTER FIVE

Having reached this stage in the book, it may seem to you that things are clear-cut, even black and white, at least in theory. But working things out in practice can be quite another matter. People's lives are complex—and circumstances may be very difficult indeed. Often there is confusion, and pain can be raw and hard to handle. So, as we walk alongside those who are affected by abortion, our own feelings can be pulled in all kinds of directions too—and we begin to wonder whether there might be some grey areas after all.

This is where we hope the next two chapters will help. Our aim is not so much to be prescriptive but rather to provide a framework within which it should be possible to navigate pastoral situations.

Identifying some foundational biblical principles will be key to this, and we'll do that in this chapter. In the next, we will look more specifically at how the principles might be applied

PRINCIPLE 1: TRUST GOD'S CHARACTER

God is love; he is good; he is powerful; and he doesn't change. The Bible describes him as compassionate and gracious (Isaiah 30 v 18), slow to anger, abounding in love and faithfulness (Psalm 86 v 15). He sees the end from the beginning (Isaiah 46 v 10) and holds everything in his hands. He promises to strengthen, help and uphold those who are afraid (Isaiah 41 v 10) and works in *all* circumstances for the good of those who love him (Romans 8 v 28). He is completely in control, and when times are hard, he promises to be our refuge and strength, an ever-present help in times of trouble (Psalm 46 v 1).

Stop and think about these truths, one at a time, phrase by phrase. They are almost too amazing to take in—but if we can do that, they will transform the way we think about even the most desperate of situations.

Consider the story of Hagar in Genesis 16. A slave-girl is pregnant with her master's (Abram's) child as a result of a plan hatched between Abram and his wife Sarai. However, Sarai becomes jealous and mistreats

Hagar, so she runs away into the desert. But God searches her out and finds her near a spring in the desert. There he speaks words of comfort and compassion and makes promises to her about the future of her unborn child.

> *[Hagar] gave this name to the Lord who spoke to her: "You are the God who sees me," for she said, "I have now seen the One who sees me." That is why the well was called Beer Lahai Roi [which means "well of the Living One who sees me"]; it is still there, between Kadesh and Bered.*　　Genesis 16 v 13-14

This story speaks directly to many of the fears that women have when unexpectedly pregnant and reveals a God who cares and draws near. It's a story that can be profoundly helpful to share with someone in turmoil over an unwanted pregnancy.

PRINCIPLE 2: REMEMBER GOD'S GRACE

We need to remember that God's ways are good—for believers and unbelievers alike. This means that, when we speak from God's word, we can be confident that it will be good for those we're speaking to—and not just for them but also for those around them and society at large. This will affect how we counsel, encourage and help family and friends. Other opinions and voices may seem louder and claim to know better, but Christians need to trust that God's ways are always the best.

Then there is forgiveness: that special kind of grace that God gives to Christians, to those who turn to him in repentance and faith. Romans 8 v 1 says, "There is now no condemnation for those who are in Christ Jesus". *Absolutely none*—because Jesus Christ took the punishment for all our sin when he died on the cross. We are washed clean and free from all guilt—including that associated with abortion and everything to do with it. What joy; what hope; what amazing grace! And that grace, once given, never fails; it continues and can sustain us through the very hardest of times.

PRINCIPLE 3: ACKNOWLEDGE THE "NOW AND NOT YET"

We live between the first and second comings of Christ. Although Jesus is Lord of all, reigning at the right hand of the Father, life is far from what it should be. Our world and everything in it is truly broken, both inside and outside the church. This means that our lives will be messy from time to time. And as we seek to help others in difficult situations, we may well find ourselves being part of solutions that are not perfect and being involved in making decisions that are not easy or clear-cut.

Not everyone will see things the way we do. In particular, while some will share our faith, others will not—and even if they do, there will still be different opinions. These result from understanding, maturity and obedience issues which will need to be considered in pastoral situations. Some young believers will make courageous faith-filled decisions; others will not. Surprisingly, some more "mature" Christians may make bad decisions. At times, choices will be made that we profoundly disagree with and even think are morally wrong. This will feel uncomfortable, but we need to continue to love and support people in such situations. All of this should be expected because we are living in the "now and not yet". We should not be surprised or discouraged. If we are, we should remember the following:

- **We are never alone or without help.** Jesus has promised that he will not leave us or forsake us (Hebrews 13:5). He has sent us his Spirit to dwell in us, to counsel and to guide. We can trust that same Spirit to be at work ahead of us as we reach out to others; and through prayer, we can seek wisdom each step of the way.
- **We always have good news to share.** The gospel of God's forgiveness and new life in Christ is a message of hope that should form the backdrop of any conversation we have and any advice we

give. Make sure the message of forgiveness is clearly heard, especially by those who may feel judged and condemned.

- **We often find rich blessing in the hardest of times.** It's one of the remarkable paradoxes of the Christian life that we often feel closer to God in hardship and suffering, and so experience him in ways we otherwise might not. And while we don't seek suffering to find such blessing, we can look to him in the midst of it. In another context, Joni Eareckson Tada (an author has been disabled with quadriplegia following an accident) captures the essence of this when she says "He has chosen not to heal me, but to hold me. The more intense the pain, the closer His embrace."[23]

PRINCIPLE 4: HAVE CONFIDENCE TO ENGAGE IN DEBATE AND CONVERSATION

So often, when we don't have all the answers, we can feel as if we have none. This may be one reason why many Christians have been slow to engage with the abortion debate and why we can sometimes be hesitant in reaching out pastorally. The fact is that there is much we can be sure of, even if we don't know or understand everything. There will always be biblical principles which we can affirm, providing

---

23 Joni Eareckson Tada, *A Place of Healing* (David C. Cook, 2015), p 40.

context and wisdom and getting us ninety percent of the way there, even if the rest remains difficult and unclear.

Recognising this, let's always seek to go forward. In the "now and not yet", we live by faith, not by sight—and even if we don't have all the answers, we are not completely in the dark or left alone. We can ask the Lord for his wisdom, his compassion and his overruling in situations. We can also seek advice from our pastors, leaders at church and other Christian friends.

PRINCIPLE 5: PREPARE FOR GOOD CONVERSATIONS

Talking about abortion can be tough, whether this is in the context of topical debate or pastoral care. Strong emotions surround the issue, and they can stop us talking about abortion and make conversations difficult when we do talk about it. It's good to be aware of this and prepare in advance when we can. The pointers below will help us do that.

- **Pray.** We sometimes forget that abortion is a spiritual issue, and so it's vital that we pray—in particular for the work of the gospel in changing hearts and minds. Pray for strength and courage to speak—and for wisdom and sensitivity when you do.

- **Be respectful and kind.** Unfortunately, we can sometimes be aggressive and accusatory in how we speak. This can be because we're judgmental; but even if it's not, it gives the appearance that it is. This is not right; neither is it helpful. 1 Peter 3 v 15 tells us to be gentle and respectful as we give reasons for the hope we have. Remember, we're *all* made in God's image—even those who we may profoundly disagree with—and the way we respond could be the thing that changes hearts and minds. Don't forget too that this may be a very personal issue and it's possible that the person you are speaking to will have had an abortion. So, while we should speak with conviction, we will need to be conscious that the person we are speaking with may have deep emotions about this subject, and so be sensitive as we speak.

- **Speak about grace.** People often fear that Christians will be judgmental, and so it's good to take the opportunity to affirm the gospel of grace. It can reassure them and help to dispel unhelpful presuppositions they might have. Consider using a short simple sentence such as "Christians believe that Jesus offers forgiveness to everyone—including those who have had an abortion". This simple statement of fact can easily be shared in conversation.

- **Tell stories.** People are always interested in the lives of others, and telling a story, particularly if it's your own, is an easy way to gain a hearing for your views, allay fears, and allow a different narrative to be heard.

- **Ask questions and be honest.** It's good to ask questions—they help you understand the other person and often reveal differences which naturally lead to further discussion. Be honest about any aspects of the *pro-life* position that perhaps you find personally difficult; it enables conversation and relationship to be genuine.

- **Don't be discouraged.** When conversations don't go well, we can tempted to be discouraged—either by our own sense of inadequacy or because, despite our best efforts, we have been rebuffed. In these situations, it's worth remembering that an empathetic, compassionate attitude can go a long way, and even when our arguments have seemed unconvincing, we can never be sure how influential they might have been. Pray and leave things to God.

MONIQUE'S STORY

Our baby was called Anjou. She had Edwards syndrome which is a chromosomal abnormality like Down syndrome, although very much worse. Only 5-10% of babies survive the first year.

Anjou's problems were first picked up on a routine antenatal scan. I was happily married to Andy, and we already had a healthy two-year-old daughter. Life was good, and we felt that nothing could go wrong.

The news about Anjou was devastating and led to the inevitable discussion with medics about terminating the pregnancy. After all, what's the point in continuing with the struggle and strife of a pregnancy where the child would not survive? But from the moment we heard the horrific news, Andy and I both felt that we wanted to continue with the pregnancy and care for our daughter until she died. It was a gut response because we believed that God was in control, and that this was a precious life that he had given to us to care for.

Anjou was born on the 18th March 2002, and four days later we took her home and cared for her until she died. We had an endless stream of visitors, many of whom cried as they held her. Sometimes it was for our pain; sometimes for theirs—such as the elderly lady who'd had multiple miscarriages and never had the opportunity to mourn. Anjou had the ability to reach deep into the lives of others, exposing pain and healing hurt.

I grew up in South Africa, and around the same time, thousands of other African women were losing their babies—this time to HIV. So we set up a charity that over the last 17 years has helped around 400,000 African children as well as their families.

Anjou, tiny and helpless, lived for only 47 days, and yet she touched and changed the lives of many. The pain is still there, but what I find so miraculous is that out of something so hard God can do something so beautiful.

ENGAGING PRACTICALLY:
COMMON QUESTIONS
CHAPTER SIX

1. Shouldn't it be a woman's right to choose what to do with her own body?

Two basic Christian truths have implications for how we think about this question. First, we are created by God. So, while we do have huge freedom and autonomy to make decisions about how we use our bodies and our minds, they do not ultimately belong to us. Rather, they belong to God and are to be used for his glory.

Second, in following Christ, Christians are called to sacrificially serve others at the expense of themselves—particularly those who are vulnerable and in need.

Elaine Storkey powerfully expresses the idea of pregnancy as hospitality and self-giving in her book *Mary's Story, Mary's Song*:

> Pregnancy itself is a symbol of deep hospitality. It is the giving of one's body to the

life of another. It is a sharing of all that we have, our cell structure, our blood stream, our food, our oxygen. It is saying "welcome" with every breath, and every heartbeat. And for many mothers that welcome is given irrespective of the demands made on one's comfort, health or ease of life. For the demands of this hospitality are greater than almost any of our own. And the growing foetus is made to know that here is love, here are warm lodgings, here is a place of safety. In hiding and in quiet the miraculous growth takes place.[24]

So, do we have a right to choose? Yes, but for Christians this should only be within the parameters of God's purposes for us. It seems like a paradox, but true freedom is only found within God's good boundaries. He is our Creator—our heavenly Father —who knows what's best for us.

But what about those who don't share the Christian faith? Submitting to God's authority would be good for everyone, with or without faith, but we cannot control what people think or do. Where abortion is legally available, women have a right to access it. But having a right in law does not make things right or wrong. Unfortunately, injustice can be legal.

---

24 Elaine Storkey, *Mary's Story, Mary's Song* (Fount, 1993) p 34.

2. My friend is unexpectedly pregnant, and she's not happy about it. She wants to talk. What should I say?

Before saying anything, make sure you listen and listen well. Don't be too quick to speak, and be prepared to give your friend lots of your time. Often, a natural sense of panic means that she may not have a clear perspective on her situation—but talking things through with you will help her process some of her emotions and perhaps prevent rash decisions.

Contemporary society offers a *quick* abortion, which might seem like a tempting solution: life gets back to "normal"; others need not know about it; medical complications are reduced, and there's an assumption that abortion, done early, is somehow "less wrong". However, this is to forget that there can be some serious physical and psychological consequences. It's therefore important to encourage your friend to be as fully informed as possible and to take time over her decision. Consider pointing her to good resources[25] and counselling organisations for additional help—having familiarised yourself with these in advance.[26]

---

25 *Pregnancy and Abortion: Your Choice* by Dr M. Houghton. A helpful and informative book in an accessible format. It takes the reader through the process of making an informed decision. You should consider reading it even if your friend doesn't.

26 See the website section on page 100.

3. My friend is seriously considering abortion. What can I say?

While professional bodies might need to be non-directive in their advice, there is more freedom within friendships to express an opinion—and, as you talk, you may well want to do this.

Explore the morality of abortion starting with questions such as *What has been your view of abortion up until now?* This might open up a conversation that only you will be able to have with your friend. You could take the opportunity to say that although you understand that it's a difficult decision, you would choose to have the child. Remember to be gentle and kind—and to speak of God's great love for her in Christ. Encourage her to trust him and "taste and see that the Lord is good" (Psalm 34 v 8).

There are three other important points: keep any conversations with your friend confidential (unless there is very good reason not to); remember to pray (for them and with them, if appropriate); and reassure your friend of your ongoing love and care—whatever decision she makes.

4. My friend has decided to have an abortion. How should I support her when I think it's wrong?

It can be hard to decide exactly how to support someone in this situation and, as Christians, we are likely to come to different decisions. On what basis do we make these? How involved should we be with our friends? Is there a line to be drawn? If so, where will it be?

In the Old Testament, Daniel knew where his line was drawn. He was happy to serve the Babylonian king, learn the language and literature (Daniel 1 v 4) and accept a new name (v 7), but he wouldn't eat royal food or drink wine (v 8). In a similar way, as we support our friend, we will want to draw lines as she goes ahead with something we profoundly disagree with. Prayerful reflection and listening to our consciences will help us decide where our particular lines are.

Those in the medical profession have had to ask themselves questions like this for years, and Christian doctors and nurses have responded differently, for different reasons. On the one hand, some have wanted to be involved, particularly in the counselling process; on the other, there are those who have not wanted to be involved at all. Sometimes this is because they have simply wanted to make a stand; sometimes, it's been a real struggle of conscience; sometimes it's due to a fear of being somehow complicit.

As we think this through for ourselves, it can be helpful to remember that while we should not sin ourselves, or lead others into it, God only holds us responsible for our own sin. We can reach out and help. Consider Jesus, who reached out to those in his day who needed help—who needed a "doctor".[27]

5. I am pregnant and against abortion in all circumstances. Should I have antenatal screening?

Significant abnormalities occur in 2-3% of children. Often these can be picked up before birth by antenatal screening, and information is helpful in enabling parents and medics to plan for any extra care a child might need. However, antenatal screening also allows women to consider abortion if there is a possibility of abnormality—something that's often viewed (including by many in the medical profession), as the responsible and obvious thing to do.

Antenatal screening is not without controversy, and ethical issues are never far away. Consider screening for Down syndrome. This initially involves a simple blood test, and few people would object to this. However, the blood test cannot tell you for certain whether you are expecting a child with Down syndrome—it will only give a probability, telling you whether you are "high-risk" or "low-risk". A definite diagnosis will only come with further tests, such as amniocentesis or chorionic villus sampling, which

---

27 See Mark 2 v 13-17

are ethically more difficult because they can induce a miscarriage: the risk of this is up to 1 in 100.

It's therefore wise to have thought through even the simplest tests in advance, asking what difference a positive (or "high-risk") result will make. Talk things through with your doctor or midwife. Listen to their advice, ask questions and express concerns. Don't be surprised if your views are different to those of others and are challenged along the way, but persevere until you're confident you have the information you need to make your decision. During the discussion you will have had a wonderful opportunity to explain, quite naturally, what you believe, allowing a *pro-life*, disability-embracing voice to be heard by people within the medical profession.

6. What about rape? Is it ok to have an abortion then?

Rape is an appalling violation. It is, though, a relatively rare reason for women to have an abortion. According to the Guttmacher Institute, the research arm of the US's leading abortion provider, Planned Parenthood, 1% of all abortions take place because of rape.[28]

In thinking about how to respond to extreme cases such as this, it is important to go back to basics—

---

28 www.bit.ly/tpabort26

including those guiding principles we discussed in the last chapter. And if we do that, the answer to this question should be clear: it is not an exception.

However conceived, the child is still a human being, created by God and loved by him. God is still sovereign, and he is still good. Nothing we face will ever change that. Of course, that does not mean that things are going to be easy, but it does mean that God can be trusted whatever tragedy comes our way in life.

We often assume that women who are raped will want an abortion. But that's not necessarily true —one study showed that 85% of women who had been raped, and had become pregnant as a result, chose to continue their pregnancy.[29]

Compounding the crime of rape with the act of abortion doesn't make things right.

JOE'S STORY

I was conceived after my mother was raped in July 1933 and I was born the following year in April 1934.

I can't begin to guess what anguish it cost my mother to be raped and then to find herself pregnant with me. And then she had to spend the long months with this undesired child that was me growing within her—and at a time when people were perhaps less

---

29 Mahkorn, "Pregnancy and Sexual Assault", *The Psychological Aspects of Abortion*, eds. Mall & Watts (University Publications of America, 1979), p 55-69.

understanding of these things than now. I do know that she suffered all of the discomfort that every pregnancy brings—along with the special shame of her situation.

But I am profoundly grateful to her that she bore me and gave me life. I was adopted the day I was born by wonderful parents, and I am here today after a long and happy life because she did give me birth.

How glad I am that abortion was not an easy option for her in the 1930s.

7. Is there ever a case for abortion?

Abortion has long been accepted when it is necessary to preserve the life of the mother—when both mother and child will die without the removal of the baby. This can happen with an ectopic pregnancy, in which the baby develops outside the uterus, usually in the Fallopian tubes. Saving one life is better than losing two.

8. I had an abortion some years ago, and I continue to feel guilty. What should i do?

This is very common, and not just for women but also for men, relatives and friends who were complicit and encouraged someone to have an abortion.

First and most importantly, you must turn to Christ—and keep doing so whenever you are tempted to doubt God's love and forgiveness. Jesus forgives, cleanses and restores you—completely—whatever your past.

Consider this courtroom scene in Isaiah. God and his people—God and you—stand face to face and yet he says:

> *"Come now, let us settle the matter…*
> *Though your sins are like scarlet,*
> *they shall be as white as snow;*
> *though they are red as crimson,*
> *they shall be like wool."*   Isaiah 1 v 18

If you have turned away from your sins and put your trust in Christ, you are acquitted in the only courtroom that really matters: all because Jesus has already paid the price that your sins deserve. In him, you are holy. God delights in you and calls you his child. You need to tell yourself this and ask God to help you trust that it's true.

Then, be patient with yourself. It can be hard to shake off feelings of guilt and shame even after you've been a Christian for some time. But maturity in the Christian life is marked by what we do with those feelings, and where we go for help, rather than whether we have them or not. So be careful not to compound any guilt by incorrect thinking. Don't listen to the devil's lies. Rather, keeping turning to Christ, trusting in his promises to you. Seek help if you need it—from a trusted friend and fellow believer at church or from professional services. Post-abortion counselling can be invaluable and is available through various Christian organisations.[30]

Also, work with God as he uses your past. He has promised that in all things he works for the good of those who love him (Romans 8 v 28)—and so you can trust him to use even your abortion for your good and his glory as you trust him. Such is his grace! Allow your love for him to grow as you realise just how much he loves you, despite everything. If you are trusting in Christ, you can be certain that before the beginning of time, Jesus set his love on you, and knowing everything there was to know about you, he chose to die for you. It's amazing how much he loves you, and nothing can change that.

God can also use your past to help others. There will be others among your family and friends, inside and outside your church community, who feel similar pain to you. Why not pray that one day you'll be able to use your experience to help them?

---

30 See the resources section on page 99.

9. Our daughter has had an abortion, and we are distraught. How can we relate positively to her and support her despite our disappointment and pain?

This is another extremely difficult and painful situation, and it's understandable that you feel distraught and sad. It's a very natural grieving process that you are going through—not just in relation to the child that has died but also related to dashed hopes and expectations you might have had for your daughter. However, there are some things it's good to remember, whatever the circumstances.

Remember that, just like the baby that has been lost, your daughter is made in the image of God and dearly loved by him. He too grieves over her choices but never stops loving her. Although it might dominate your thinking at the moment, her abortion does not define her, and there is much that is good and beautiful about her that you can give thanks for. We live in this seemingly irreconcilable tension in the "now and not yet".

Remember too your own need for grace. Our sinfulness is profound, and our forgiveness in Christ is completely undeserved. So seek to reach out to your daughter as Christ reached out to you—out of an appreciation of the grace you have received.[31]

The sooner you reach out, the better—it's easier and avoids the topic becoming a no-go area between you—but please be very sensitive and don't force the issue. In the time immediately after the abortion, show your daughter that you care for her physical health and ask appropriate questions such as *How do you feel? Is everything getting back to normal?* If she needs further medical attention, be sure you're available to help her.

Further down the line, if she seems to be struggling emotionally, don't be afraid to gently ask, *Do you think this might have anything to do with the abortion?* and support her if she needs particular help, including post-abortion counselling.

Make a mental note of when the baby would have been born; that can be a particularly difficult time. And, as appropriate, remind your daughter of God's love for her and the forgiveness he offers her in Christ. You will, though, need to be very sensitive about all this, while being prepared to step in and help at any time at her invitation.

Beware of blaming yourself for what has happened. Asking *Where did we go wrong?* seldom helps. God's forgiveness is past, present and future

---

31 Julia Marsden's book *Forgiveness* (10Publishing, 2014) might help if you are finding this difficult.

for those who put their faith in Christ. As you reflect on this for yourself, pray that your daughter would know this too.

10. What about contraception and fertility treatment?

The principles we have discussed certainly have a bearing on issues of contraception. Contraceptives work in various ways: often, even if it is not their primary mode of action, they have the potential to prevent implantation and so induce a very early abortion. Do ask your doctor about how the contraceptive they are prescribing works and whether it *has the potential to stop implantation*. Generally speaking, doctors work on the assumption that life begins at implantation rather than fertilisation and so, for them, it is not an ethical problem to interrupt natural processes pre-implantation—so be prepared to be clear in your discussions. The situation with emergency contraception, which has traditionally been thought to cause pre-implantation abortions, is more nuanced with newer methods; again, discuss the details with your doctor and ask questions about the ethics of particular methods.

Sometimes people raise the issue of the early embryos which pass through the uterus without ever implanting. Indeed, this does take place, but that doesn't mean we can take deliberate action to make it happen. There is a difference between things that occur "naturally" in this fallen world, and us intervening to ensure that they do.

The area of fertility treatment is fraught with ethical dilemmas: consider, for instance, standard IVF treatment, where, in our society, literally millions of embryos are produced, frozen and then left on ice indefinitely. Christians will need to think, pray and carefully discuss the options available to them. It is true to say that people make different decisions in this area. For a variety of reasons (not just ethical ones), some decide not to have IVF at all and consider alternatives such as adoption and fostering. Others modify the usual treatment process: for example, by limiting the number of embryos produced and the number introduced back into the womb, thereby giving each embryo created the best possible chance of life.

11. Do you have any advice for talking to non-christian friends about abortion?

Opportunities often arise to talk about abortion, especially when it is in the news. Whether it's a proposed change in legislation or a particularly difficult and tragic situation, there is something you can say in conversation. Don't forget to express sympathy where that's appropriate and ask questions to encourage discussion.

There are two things to bear in mind as you talk:

- **Don't be afraid of exposing contradictions in society or in *pro-choice* arguments.** We have discussed some of these in this book. Whether it's around the use of health-care resources or our attitudes to disability and gender, it is worth pointing out how our world often doesn't make sense. Be prepared to highlight the dangers of personhood arguments. In addition, you might challenge the assumption that *pro-choice* is really *pro-choice* because some would argue that it's the *pro-life* lobby who are really *pro-choice* since it is often they who are prepared to discuss options other than abortion and to support women in their decisions. The documentary *HUSH*, which is made by *pro-choice* supporters, makes the point that rarely are people who have an abortion given all the facts, making it impossible for them to make a truly informed choice.[32]

- **Help people to see and understand what's really going on.** Many just don't realise the extent and realities of abortion practice, or, if they do, they are in denial. People are often shocked, for instance, when they realise just how many

32 See hushfilm.com

abortions there are, so mention some statistics. Reclaim language by referring to the child *in utero* as *he* or *she*, instead of *it*. Get to know what a baby is like at what stage of gestation so that you can create visual images in conversation. Sometimes, though, words are unnecessary because real images can be very powerful; showing people what a 13-week-old baby looks like is evidence that does not need a conversation to do its work.[33]

People you are speaking to may well assume that Christian convictions underpin your thinking, so take any opportunity to speak about Christ. Remember, too, that abortion is very common and it may be a very personal issue for those you're speaking to. Therefore, consider emphasising that people often think of Christians as judgmental on this issue but the truth is that Jesus welcomes everyone. Be prepared to share the gospel.

12. I am a man who is frustrated that, so often, abortion is seen as a woman's issue. How can my voice be heard?

33 Many websites show images of normal pregnancy (https://www.youtube.com/watch?v=l1qvUPYDnOY). Some Christians advocate the use of images of aborted babies (https://www.cbruk.org/abortionreality). The two side by side are shocking. Watch these yourself and be prepared to talk about them or refer friends to them.

In public debate, abortion is seen as a women's issue, closely linked to women's rights. It's understandable why this is the case. Women carry the consequences of an unplanned pregnancy in a way that men never will. By and large they, not men, also carry the responsibility for childcare. So it is perhaps understandable that women have sometimes denied men a voice. Nevertheless, it is important that the voices of men who speak and live by God's loving truth are heard in a range of areas:

- In respecting and honouring women and their bodies. Ever since the fall the tendency has been for women to be subjugated by men. We see it still today in the selective abortion of female babies, in human trafficking, in the #MeToo scandals and the like. This is not right. Christian men should be powerful and vociferous advocates for the honouring, respect and protection of women.
- In the area of sex, marriage and family life. So that pregnancies, if unplanned, occur in the context of loving commitment and support.
- In accepting the consequences of unplanned pregnancy that they have been responsible for and supporting the woman in this situation.

It would be remiss not to acknowledge the pain caused to men by abortion, either when they have had to stand by as a child of theirs has been aborted or as a result of the guilt they have felt having coerced someone into having an abortion. Much of what has been said in this chapter about guilt and forgiveness applies to men as well as women.

13. What can we be doing as a church on this issue?

We need to remember that, fundamentally, the gospel message about Jesus is the solution that we need—both as individuals and as a wider society. It is a vital message of forgiveness and hope, and it's crucial that our churches continue to preach it and teach it clearly. As people hear the gospel and respond to it, healing happens and change takes place.

However, in view of the enormous pain and injustice of abortion, there are some specific things we should do:

- Make ourselves aware of what is going on, both in our churches and in the wider world. Church leaders have a particular responsibility in this area.
- Equip ourselves to talk wisely and compassionately.
- Create a church culture where people feel they can speak to others about issues they're struggling with, including unwanted pregnancy or past abortion. The public sharing of relevant testimonies is a powerful way of doing this.

- Know where help can be found. Sometimes this will be within your church; sometimes this will involve pointing people to outside groups and organisations.
- Support others as they campaign for legislative change.
- Consider other practical responses and pray about what this might involve.

In practice, small things can help: displaying appropriate leaflets (for example, about Christian counselling organisations); stocking suitable books on your bookstall; advertising events run by *pro-life* groups and encouraging people to support them.

Pastors and local church leaders, however, are in a powerful position and their voices need to be heard on this issue. There are many ways they might do this: from the sensitive referencing of abortion in a sermon to a specific teaching session designed to inform and educate church members. These initiatives will help to dispel any stigma and break the silence, motivating Christians to engage with others on this issue wisely and compassionately.

14. How should we understand Exodus 21 v 22-24?

These verses refer to a penalty for accidentally causing injury to a pregnant woman and/or her child and, depending on what translation of the Bible you read, they might appear to contradict some of what's been said in this book. *Pro-choice* campaigners and others often draw attention to them. The fact is that there is ambiguity in the original Hebrew over whether the text refers to a miscarriage or premature birth—and whether it's injury to the child or the mother that's in view. Either way, accidental injury is being referred to— not the deliberate causing of harm.

APPENDIX 1
HOW ABORTION IS PERFORMED

The information below is based on current practice in the UK, but it is not dissimilar in other parts of the world. Abortion is performed either medically or surgically.

SURGICAL ABORTION

Up to 15 weeks gestation: Vacuum aspiration under local or general anaesthetic. In this procedure the cervix may be dilated, by passing dilators of increasing diameter through it, before a suction tube is inserted into the uterus to remove the embryo/foetus.

Between 15 and 22/24 weeks gestation: Dilatation and evacuation—which is more likely to be performed under general anaesthetic. Forceps are passed through a dilated cervix to remove the foetus from the uterus; the foetus is usually broken up in the process—identifiable body parts being removed one after another. Sometimes the head is deliberately crushed so that it can pass through the cervix.

MEDICAL ABORTION

This can be performed up to 22/24 weeks gestation. First, a tablet of mifepristone is taken. This breaks down the lining of the uterus and the foetus dies. 24-48 hours later, when at home, a second drug (misoprostol) is taken by mouth or as a vaginal pessary. Strong contractions occur, and the foetus is expelled and usually passed into the toilet. Bleeding can be heavy and the process very painful—both physically and emotionally.

FOETICIDE
Carried out after 22 weeks gestation. The foetus is given a lethal injection and then labour is induced.

APPENDIX 2
MISCARRIAGE: A STRANGE
AND LONELY GRIEF

Much of what's been said in this book will have a bearing on how we view miscarriage. It's thought that one in four known pregnancies ends in loss, which means, undoubtedly, that a significant number of people in our church congregations will have known the pain of miscarriage.

When a miscarriage has happened later in pregnancy or there's been a stillbirth, the emotional pain is likely to be especially acute, but it is significant whenever it occurs. The result can be a very strange kind of grief, because the parents are mourning someone they've never met. And it can be a very lonely grief because it's often unknown or unnoticed by others.

Those who are seeking to support friends who have had this experience must be careful not to minimise the loss that people have experienced— either in their words or in their attitude towards them. A couple become parents at the moment of conception, and then, God willing, they will meet their child at birth. So, the couple are genuinely grieving the loss of a child.

Some have found comfort in gathering a group of friends for a time of prayer, or in organising and conducting a simple funeral service. A number of people have found Jack Hayford's short book *I'll Hold You in Heaven* a great help and encouragement.

APPENDIX 3
THE GOSPEL OF RECONCILIATION

This is a wonderful message of hope for all of us—personally and when tempted to despair—as we look at the world around us. The life, death and resurrection of Jesus Christ really does change everything. For everyone.

Colossians 1 v 19-23 says this about Jesus:

> [19]*For God was pleased to have all his fullness dwell in him,* [20]*and through him to reconcile to himself all things, whether things on earth or things in heaven, by making peace through his blood, shed on the cross.*
>
> [21]*Once you were alienated from God and were enemies in your minds because of your evil behaviour.* [22]*But now he has reconciled you by Christ's physical body through death to present you holy in his sight, without blemish and free from accusation—*[23]*if you continue in your faith, established and firm, and do not move from the hope held out in the gospel.*

The point is clear from these verses: God longs for reconciliation—reconciliation between himself and his broken world (v 20), and between himself and each one of us individually (v 22). And the good news is that everything necessary has been done to achieve it. When Jesus died on the cross 2,000 years ago, he gave his life for us. The punishment we deserved was taken by him so that, through faith, we could be "holy in his sight, without blemish and free from accusation" (v 22): forgiven and free.

That is wonderful news when we are burdened by guilt and shame. It's also wonderful news when we feel helpless as we look at the world around us. One day everything will be put right.

For more information about what Christians believe and why they believe it, visit www.christianityexplored.org.

RESOURCES

Books

- John Wyatt, *Matters of Life and Death* (IVP, 2009)
- Dr Meghan Best, *Fearfully and Wonderfully Made* (Matthias Media, 2012)
- Daniel Darling, *The Dignity Revolution* (The Good Book Company, 2018)
- John R. W. Stott, *Issues Facing Christians Today* (Zondervan, 2006)
- Dr M. Houghton, *Pregnancy and Abortion: Your Choice* (Malcolm Down Publishing, 2017)
- Nancy Pearcey: *Love Thy Body* (Baker Books, 2018)
- Sue Ellen Browder: *Subverted (How I helped the Sexual Revolution Hijack the Women's Movement)* (Ignatius Press, 2015)
- Angela Lanfranchi, Ian Gentles, Elizabeth Ring-Cassidy, *Complications: Abortion's Impact on Women* (The deVeber Institute for Bioethics and Social Research, 2015)
- Julia Marsden, *Forgiveness* (10Publishing, 2014)
- Jack Hayford *I'll Hold You in Heaven* (Chosen Books, 2015)
- Joni Eareckson Tada, *A Place of Healing* (David C. Cook, 2015)
- Elaine Storkey, *Mary's Story, Mary's Song* (Fount, 1993)

Documentaries

- hushfilm.com. A *pro-choice* film that honestly investigates the effects of abortion on women.
- www.stringsattachedfilm.com. This film highlights how Western governments and donor agencies tie international aid to abortion rights. It allows an African, rather than a Western, voice to be heard on the issue.

Websites and agencies

UK

- **Life:** Counselling, support and advocacy. lifecharity.org.uk
- **Pregnancy Choices:** A directory of Christian crisis-pregnancy centres. pregnancychoicesdirectory.com
- **Society for the Unborn Child:** Mainly Christian advocacy. spuc.org.uk
- **CARE:** A Christian agency that conducts research and advocacy in a variety of areas including abortion. www.care.org.uk
- **PCN:** Support and training for those running independent pregnancy centres. pregnancycentresnetwork.org.uk

USA

- **ERLC:** The Ethics and Religious Liberties Commission champions a number of initiatives relating to abortion. erlc.com
- **Stand for Life:** An ERLC website filled with stories about choosing life over abortion. standforlife.org
- **Heartbeat International:** Training for pregnancy resource centers. heartbeatinternational.org
- **Carenet:** Training for pregnancy resource centres. care-net.org
- **Human Coalition:** Pregnancy resource centre. humancoalition.org
- **Live Action:** Advocacy organisation. liveaction.org
- **Embrace Grace:** Care for single mothers. embracegrace.com
- **Focus on the Family:** focusonthefamily.com/pro-life

ABORTION
DISCUSSION GUIDE

This series does not aim to say everything there is to say about a subject, but to give an overview and a solid grounding to Christians who are starting to think about the issue from the Bible. We hope that as you discuss this book, and the Bible passages that it is based on, you will gain confidence to speak faithfully, compassionately and wisely to others.

Below is a list of questions. Please pick and choose the ones that suit your group and the time you have available. If you are leading a group discussion, try to keep constantly in people's minds that this is not simply a conversation about a political or moral "issue" that is "out there". It is an issue that is very much "in here". There are likely to be people in your church who have had an abortion, or who have been touched by one at some stage—a father, sibling, grandparent, and so on. And there may be people who are, or will be in the future, feeling the pressure to have an abortion. How we think, react to, talk and teach about this subject will help shape the culture of our churches. It will determine how well we care for people within them and how we relate to the wider non-Christian culture.

TO START

- What is your immediate reaction to the idea of talking or even thinking about abortion as a subject?
- What attitudes have you heard expressed about abortion from other people? What do you think are some of the positives and negatives in regard to each of these viewpoints?
- Why do you think we find abortion so difficult to discuss?

CHAPTER 1: WHERE ARE WE?

- Take a moment to reflect privately on ways in which you have been personally affected by abortion. How might this influence the way you think about this issue. Share any thoughts you'd like to.
- What language do you use about pregnancy and the child in the womb. Why are the words we use so powerful?
- Are you aware of the specific laws relating to abortion in your country, and any modifications made to it by your state or region?
- What are the drivers you see behind those who adopt a *pro-life* or *pro-choice* stance? What do you see as positive and negative about those motivations?
- What are your thoughts about sex-selective abortion?
- What challenges does it present to know that there will be some people, perhaps many, in your congregations who have been affected by abortion in some way or other?

CHAPTER 2: WHO ARE WE?

- Why is the Christian view of creation so fundamental to how we think about this issue?
- What do you take from Beth's story on page 35 that will help you relate more compassionately towards those affected by abortion?

CHAPTER 3: WHEN ARE WE HUMAN?

- How do Psalm 139 and the Gospel narratives about Jesus' birth help us see more clearly the truth that life begins at conception?
- How might you explain this viewpoint to someone who does not share a Christian view of the world?
- What different views are there on when human person-hood begins? What is the problem with each of them?

CHAPTER 4: A COMPLEX ISSUE

- What makes you reticent to speak about abortion as an issue to others? How might you overcome that?
- How does the diagram on page 52 help you to see what a fully rounded Christian response to the abortion issue should be?
- Are there any areas you feel drawn to get involved in?

CHAPTER 5: ENGAGING PRACTICALLY:
SOME GUIDING PRINCIPLES

- Talk through the five principles in this chapter. Which of these do you most need to be convinced of at the moment?
- How is the story of Hagar helpful in reassuring those in turmoil over an unwanted pregnancy?
- The "now and not yet" principle is important for being realistic about what we can achieve. How does it help us if we are pessimistic? How can it help us if we are too optimistic?
- What do you take from Monique's story on pages 68-69? How can telling positive stories of those who have rejected abortion help our discussions with others?

CHAPTER 6: ENGAGING PRACTICALLY:
APPLYING THE PRINCIPLES

- Talk through each of the questions in this chapter. What would your best outcome be for the people concerned? What would you find most difficult to do or say?
- In the scenario described in section 4 on page 75, where would you draw the line?
- What steps do you think you should make as a church to engage more fully in this area?

TO FINISH

- What's the big thing that has impacted you from reading this book?
- How will you now think differently about and pray for those who are considering an abortion, or are affected by it in some way?
- What extra help, training and information do you think you need to be better equipped in discussing this issue with others?

PRAY

- Ask God to help you understand the issues around abortion and the people involved with it better.
- Pray that your church fellowship would be a place where people find the freedom to talk about their struggles with this so-often secret issue. Pray that they would be taught, supported and encouraged to seek forgiveness and peace in Christ.
- Pray for campaigning and support agencies that are practically involved in working to educate, advocate and offer practical counselling services to those considering abortion.

Printable copies of this discussion guide are available at:
www.thegoodbook.co.uk/talking-points-abortion
www.thegoodbook.com/talking-points-abortion

ACKNOWLEDGEMENTS

Thank you to all those who shared their stories in this book. We are grateful, too, to Fiona Jani, Nancy-Page Lowenfield, Pete Wilkinson, Eve Hitchens, Matt Pope, Josh and Claire Hordern, and Jenny Baines for reading various drafts and making many helpful comments. Tim Thornborough has, once again, been a great editor—it truly was a team effort.

A TALKING POINTS BOOK BY
VAUGHAN ROBERTS

TRANSGENDER

There's been huge cultural change in the last few decades. Same-sex marriage would have been unthinkable 20 or 30 years ago. Now it's almost universally accepted in the Western world. Suddenly the issue of transgender is the next big social, cultural issue that is dominating the headlines.

Vaughan Roberts surveys the Christian worldview and seeks to apply the principles that he uncovers to the many complex questions surrounding gender identity. This short book gives an overview and a starting point for constructive discussion as we seek to live in a world with different values, and to love, serve and relate to transgender people.

Talking Points is a series of short books designed to help Christians think and talk about today's big issues, and to relate to others with compassion, conviction and wisdom.

> "In this brief book on a complex subject Vaughan
> Roberts combines the traditional Christian understanding of
> gender and the body with a very careful, loving, understanding
> stance toward transgender people. The two almost never go
> together, and that's why this book is so good!"
> Tim Keller, pastor and author

A TALKING POINTS BOOK BY
VAUGHAN ROBERTS

TRANSGENDER

thegoodbook.co.uk | thegoodbook.com
thegoodbook.com.au | thegoodbook.co.nz | thegoodbook.co.in

A TALKING POINTS BOOK BY
VAUGHAN ROBERTS

ASSISTED SUICIDE

There is a growing move in many parts of the world to legalise assisted suicide: allowing doctors to help end someone's life if that person so desires. What are Christians supposed to think about this issue, and how do we talk about it, and face these issues personally?

In this short book, Vaughan Roberts briefs Christians on the complex questions surrounding assisted suicide and the choices we face at the end of our lives. He surveys the Christian worldview and helps us to apply its principles as we navigate life and death in a society with contrasting values.

Talking Points is a series of short books designed to help Christians think and talk about today's big issues, and to relate to others with compassion, conviction and wisdom.

> *"This little book is a very helpful resource for anyone coming to consider the difficult question of the place of human choice at the end of life for the first time. With a tone both sensitive and authentic in its shaping by personal experience, Roberts offers an erudite yet accessible survey of an issue set only to increase in significance."*
>
> Andrew Moore, Apologist for the Zacharias Trust and Director of the RZIM Festival of Thought

A TALKING POINTS BOOK BY
VAUGHAN ROBERTS

ASSISTED SUICIDE

thegoodbook.co.uk | thegoodbook.com
thegoodbook.com.au | thegoodbook.co.nz | thegoodbook.co.in

thegoodbook
COMPANY

BIBLICAL | RELEVANT | ACCESSIBLE

At The Good Book Company, we are dedicated to helping Christians and local churches grow. We believe that God's growth process always starts with hearing clearly what he has said to us through his timeless word—the Bible.

Ever since we opened our doors in 1991, we have been striving to produce Bible-based resources that bring glory to God. We have grown to become an international provider of user-friendly resources to the Christian community, with believers of all backgrounds and denominations using our books, Bible studies, devotionals, evangelistic resources, and DVD-based courses.

We want to equip ordinary Christians to live for Christ day by day, and churches to grow in their knowledge of God, their love for one another, and the effectiveness of their outreach.

Call us for a discussion of your needs or visit one of our local websites for more information on the resources and services we provide.

Your friends at The Good Book Company

thegoodbook.com | thegoodbook.co.uk
thegoodbook.com.au | thegoodbook.co.nz
thegoodbook.co.in